Race, Reflect, Realise

Dharmin Harish Thakkar

India | USA | UK

Dedication

To you, the one who picked up this book.
Maybe you found it, maybe it found you.
May these pages bring you the reflection, comfort, or
clarity you seek.

Preface

"Why do we keep running after things that never feel enough? Why do we hold on to what we know won't last? Why do we wait for the right time to truly live?"

This book is not an answer - it's an invitation - to pause, reflect, and see the unseen truths in everyday life. These poems are born from moments of realisation, quiet observations, and the questions we often don't stop to ask. Some may challenge your perspective, some may bring comfort, and some may simply remind you of things you've always known but forgotten.

You may not resonate with every word, and that's okay. Take what speaks to you, leave what doesn't, and let the rest find you when the time is right.

So, as you turn these pages, I hope you find a piece of yourself in them. More importantly, I hope they remind you to truly live - before the moment slips away.

Acknowledgements

No book is ever written alone, and this one is no exception.

To my family and friends, thank you for being my constant support, for the conversations that turned into poetry, and for always believing in me.

To the experiences, the fleeting moments, and even the struggles - thank you for shaping these words.

To every reader who picks up this book - thank you for allowing these poems to be a part of your journey. Your time, your thoughts, and your reflections mean more than words can say.

To technology, specifically AI, which served as a tool in my process - helping refine my words while ensuring my voice remained true.

And to the unspoken stories, the unanswered questions, and the beauty of life itself - this book exists because of you.

The Architect of My Journey

A book of poetry is often a reflection of one's heart, a canvas where emotions take shape in words. As I embark on this journey, it feels only right to begin with the man who has been my first teacher, my strongest pillar, and my guiding star - my Father.

This first poem is a deeply personal tribute to him.

If you wish, feel free to start here or skip to the next section—whether you're here for a quiet thought, a gentle reminder, or a fresh perspective. There's something here for everyone.

To me, my father is more than just a parent. He is my godfather, my mentor, and my greatest source of inspiration. His wisdom, patience, and unwavering strength have shaped me in ways I cannot fully articulate. He is a man of many roles - an engineer, a businessman, a mentor, and a friend to many. But to me, he is the one who has always stood by my side, offering silent yet profound guidance. The poem is a celebration of his life, his journey, and his indomitable spirit.

Maestro DAD

Jai Shree Krushna, Papa,
Trying to express my love in your own style.
A person like you
Deserves the world's utmost happiness and smiles.

Harish, Papa, Motapapa, Bhai, Mama:
All your names.
A blind trust in you,
You stood in our lives like a crane.

Thakkars, Somaiyas, Morzarias, Karias issues,
You are always first to assist.
Ways you've aided one and all
Would make an endless list.

You were not faster than a cheetah, yet, swiftly,
You always came to your brother's defence.
You may not wholly help your brothers to sell policies or
flats,

But you lifted their spirits when their lives made no
sense.

You did not have webs in your palms, no masks, no
rings, no wings,
Nor any supernatural power.
But ask your sisters,
They'll always say, "Harish is always there in our darkest
hour."

Many times, the world placed you in a maze,
Many times, you were not supported by your own men.
But you always told us,
"It was all Thakorji's own plan."

Your knowledge, wisdom, instincts showed the way,
We are fortunate to have your blessings every day.
No one may tell you how important you are,
In our cosmos, you are the brightest star.

From Ba to Saloni, we proclaim,
Your life was not a child's game.
Your vibes are super strong,
And taught us what is right and what is wrong.

In your 30s you woke up before sunrise,
Guided Tejas, Pankit and me,

To play cricket at SAI,
Even when the sacrifice came at a price.

In your 50s you woke up before sunrise,
Guided your customers and clients
To get Umergaon's best price,
All these years, your hard work hasn't diminished.

The Godrej days,
Hopping between hardware stores day-to-day.
Smiling, loving, caring,
Silently facing struggles on your way.

Remembering your duty — to LIC, to us — with a tired
face,
Travelling across Mumbai in Kinetic, your daily race.
You earned immense gold and fame,
We know how 'Dil se' you played the game.

You followed your passion,
Travelling to Umergaon night and day.
Finally, you got your piece of a huge terrace,
A dream no one could take away.

From Engineer to Manufacturer, to Distributor, to LIC, to
Estate Consultant —
We've all seen.

And everyone who knows you says,
"Harish is evergreen."

You are the pillar, the strength of the Thakkar family,
The reason behind our smiles.
You know how much we all love you,
Deep down, you've always been our guide.

The phone rings — "Dad" pops up.
Not a second wasted, the call gets picked up.
Your video calls are my shelter,
Reassuring me, making everything better.

Your life, your lessons - you may think I didn't see,
You may think I didn't hear,
But trust me, Papa
I didn't miss even a single vibe and ear.

From Pulsar to i20 to iPhones,
You've gifted me all.
I promise – I'll give you all happiness,
Till my last fall.

I relive all times spent together,
The moments shared, the lessons you gave.
My God, my star — you are,
I pledge that I won't go too far.

I bow for any failure,
When times were bad,
My worship will be eternal,
Because you are my "MAESTRO DAD."

This poem attempts to encapsulate a lifetime of gratitude, love, and admiration. While words may never fully capture what a father means to his child, I hope this serves as a humble expression of my deepest feelings. Through this book, as I share my thoughts with the world, I want to begin with the one person who has shaped my world.

Love you a lot, Papa.

Timeless Lessons from Life

Some lessons never age. They are the unspoken truths we often overlook, the wisdom we have known as humans forever, but we realise it only when we pause. This section captures those timeless reflections - simple yet profound realisations that shape our journey of life.

The Beauty of Beginnings

A blank page, untouched and white,
A chance to start new, bold and bright.
Just like a bird that learns to fly,
The first flap is unsure, but it touches the sky.

Like a seed planted deep in the earth,
It grows, unaware of its own worth.
From humble beginnings, a tree will rise,
With roots in the soil and branches to the skies.

The first step is always the hardest to take,
It's all about the leap we make.
So here I stand, taking the leap,
With words I sow, thoughts so deep,

Not knowing where this path will go,
But proud of this start, that much I know.
This marks the start of my poetic way,
A simple beginning, but here to stay.

Reflection - *Every journey begins with a first step. The hardest part is to start, but once we do, the path unfolds.*
What's stopping you from starting?

Stay Curious

A child gazes at the endless sky,
Asking questions, with curious eye.
Why do stars shine? Where does the wind go?
So much to see, so much to know.

They touch the rain, they chase the breeze,
They wonder why leaves fall from trees.
They ask and ask, they want to know,
Their world is big, it seems to grow.

But as we age, we start to hide,
We stop the questions deep inside.
We rush, we work, we play it safe,
Forgetting wonder, losing faith.

Yet those who ask and seek to learn,
Find new paths at every turn.
So keep that spark, don't let it fade,
Let questions be the path you pave.
For those who wonder, dream, and strive,

Will always rise, will always fly.

Reflection - *Children ask endless questions, but as we grow, we stop wondering and we hide our questions. Curiosity is the key to a life well lived.*
When was the last time you truly questioned something? Remember the times when you were a child, filled with wonder and curiosity?
Let that spark guide you to new discoveries.

The Weight of a Word

One word can cut deeper than a sword.
A whisper can heal more than a speech.
Yet, we throw them carelessly into the air,
Not thinking if they harm or care.

Unspoken, Yet Needed

We say "thank you" in emails, polite and neat,
To colleagues we pass, to strangers we meet.
But have we thanked the ones who stay,
Who love us through every joy and gray?

We say "sorry" when we bump on the street,
Or when a deadline we fail to meet.
But have we said it to those we've wronged,
To those who stayed along?

We speak with ease where it barely stays,
But hold back where it truly weighs.
The ones who raised, who wiped our tears,
Wait for words they've missed for years.

So before the moment slips away,
Say what your heart has longed to say.
Not just to those who pass you by,
But to the ones who'll stand till the last goodbye.

Reflection - *We thank strangers, but forget to express gratitude to those who love us the most. We say sorry where it barely matters, but hold back where it does.* **Have you told the people who matter how much they truly mean to you? Take a moment to reflect on your relationships. Who in your life deserves a heartfelt 'thank you' or 'sorry' today?**

Last Seen: 10 Years Ago

Once, it was new, shiny, and bright,
Now it sits in a box, out of sight.
The watch we cherished, worn every day,
Now gathers dust, tucked away.

The jacket we chose with such great care,
Now untouched, yet still lying there.
A childhood toy, once held so tight,
Now forgotten, out of sight.

We buy and store, thinking they'll stay,
Yet time moves on, and they fade away.
What truly matters, we should embrace,
Not just collect, then lose in the race

Reflection - *Not everything we buy will hold meaning forever. Treasure what carries memories, but pause before adding more.*
Are you preserving what matters, or just accumulating things that time will erase?

Patience in Nature's Way

The eagle soars with no rush in sight,
It waits for the wind to catch its flight.
With wings spread wide, it takes its time,
A gentle reminder that the right moment will align.

The turtle moves slow, but steady and sure,
Its path is long, but its journey is pure.
It doesn't hurry, no race to win,
It teaches us that patience comes from within.

In nature, the lesson is clear and true,
Patience isn't weakness; it helps us break through.
Like the eagle in the sky, the turtle on the ground,
Sometimes the best way forward is to stand still and be
found.

Reflection - *Nature teaches us patience - the eagle waits
for the right wind, the tree takes years to grow. Life
unfolds at its own pace.* **Are you trusting the process, or
are you rushing the outcome?**

The Quiet Power of Growth

We don't always see growth as it happens. It unfolds in small steps, in silent transformations, and in the kindness we offer. These poems reflect how persistence, unseen change, and selfless giving shape who we become.

One Step at a Time

A Badminton player stands, racket in hand,
The final score is not the plan.
Forget the scoreboard, play each point,
One by one, they all will join.

A climber walks a mountain tall,
The peak seems far, the path too long.
But one small step, then one more,
And soon they stand where eagles soar.

A chess player scans the board,
The final checkmate seems too far.
But one good move, then one more,
First principles, the path unfolds.

We search for endings, far and wide,
Yet all we need is the next small guide.
Don't chase the future, don't fear the climb,
Just take the next step - it's all in time.

Reflection - *Big goals feel overwhelming, but every journey is just a series of small steps. Progress is made by moving forward, even if slowly.*
Are you focusing on the next step or only on the finish line?

The Unseen Growth

Milk can go bad, but don't fear,
It turns to yogurt, richer and clear.
If it stays longer, it turns to cheese,
More valuable than milk, aged to please.

Grape juice can sour, it's not the end,
It turns to wine, more expensive, my friend.
What seemed ruined, what seemed wrong,
Becomes more precious as time goes on.

Let's not fear mistakes or changes we see,
They don't break us, they set us free.
With each step, with every try,
We're not broken, we're learning to fly.

Reflection - *What feels like failure is often transformation. The best things take time to evolve.* **Are you seeing setbacks as endings or as beginnings in disguise?**

Someone Lives When Someone Gives

A smile to a stranger, a hand to hold,
A little bit of kindness, a heart that's bold.
When we help someone, or lift them high,
We make them stronger, we help them fly.

It's not about money or things we own,
But the love we share and how it's shown.
A kind word spoken, a friend in need,
A small act of kindness plants a seed.

The smallest gesture can heal a wound,
A warm meal shared, a shoulder to lean.
In giving, we find a way to grow,
Someone lives when love starts to flow.

So give what we can, and give it with grace,
In every small act, we brighten a face.
The world feels lighter, hearts start to shine,
Someone lives when we make them fine.

Reflection - *Kindness is the simplest, yet most powerful gift. A small act of giving can change someone's world.* **What can you give today to someone that costs nothing but means everything?**

Illusions We Live By

Life often feels like a game of control, ownership, and certainty—but is it? This section challenges the illusions we build, the false assurances we hold, and the truths we struggle to accept.

The Illusion of Control

We think we control the path we take,
That every step is ours to make.
But life moves in ways we can't see,
And sometimes, we must let things be.

We hold the kite, its string so tight,
Believing we control its flight.
Yet winds decide where it will soar,
And we just follow, nothing more

We plant a seed and think we make it grow,
But it's the rain, the soil, the sun that really know.
We water it, we wait, but nature's the one in control,
And we watch, as time plays its role

We chase the idea, thinking we steer the way,
But like the kite, the seed, life has its say.
So let go of little control and enjoy the ride,
For we're just passengers, with life as our guide.

***Reflection** - We think we control life, but in reality, life moves on its own path. The more we try to grip tightly, the more we struggle.*

Are you steering your life, or is life steering you? What would happen if you let go a little?

The Illusion of More

The passionate dream of shining bright,
While the famous hide from the light.

The young wish to grow up fast,
While the old long for the past.

The student dreams of a job one day,
While workers wish for school's old play.

The poor hope for riches and gold,
While the rich miss the peace they sold.

We chase and chase, yet fail to see,
Happiness hides in what already is.

The grass looks greener far away,
But it only grows where we choose to stay.

If we stop and take a look,
We'll find more blessings than we took.

No one has it all, but all have enough,
If only we stopped comparing so much.

Take a breath, be still, be true,
And thank life for what it gave you.

Reflection - *We always think happiness is in the next achievement, the next possession. But the real joy is already here.* **Are you chasing more or appreciating enough?**

Illusion of Permanent Address

We build and stretch, chasing dreams so wide,
To create a home where we can reside.
But what we create may not last through time,
A house sold, or fought for, or replaced in its prime.

A house is not just bricks and land,
But laughter, love, and a helping hand.
Yet we spend our years in endless chase,
Trying to own, yet losing space.

Why do we stretch to get permanent ownership,
Where our life is only leased,
With an uncertain tenure given by a landlord,
Whose terms are final with no court appeal?

Every time I fill a form,
And see "Permanent Address" written,
I smile at what we fail to see -
Is it really permanent in this leased life of mine?

So build with love, and live with ease,
But don't let chase steal the peace.
For no matter how high we raise the walls,
The best moments happen beyond them all.

Reflection: *We build homes, we claim spaces, but in the grand scheme of time, nothing belongs to us. Everything is temporary, including us. Building a home is beautiful, but when we stretch too far - giving up happiness, time, and peace in the process we lose more than we gain.* **Are you building wisely? What truly makes a place yours - the walls or the moments?**

The Illusion of Power

The lion, strong and full of might,
Rules the jungle, day and night.
It chases, hunts, and wins the race,
Living with power and setting the pace.

But time moves on, and things change fast,
The lion grows old, its strength won't last.
Once fierce and bold, now slow and weak,
The roar it had is now hard to speak.

The hyenas circle, ready to feast,
The lion is helpless, no longer a beast.
The time has come, the end is near,
Even the mighty must face their fear.

Beauty fades, and strength will go,
One day, we all will feel it too.
Let's be humble, and help those in need,
For one day, we too will no longer lead.

Reflection: *Strength and dominance fade with time. Even the mightiest eventually fall.*

Are you using your power wisely, knowing it won't last forever?

Wisdom We Forgot

Sometimes, progress makes us forget the wisdom of the past. Whether it's traditions, connections, or values, we often dismiss what once anchored us. These poems reflect on what we have left behind—and what we might need to reclaim.

Old Roots, New Names

They laughed at haldi doodh, called it old-school,
Now it's a turmeric latte, trendy and cool.

Fasting on Ekadashi was seen as a chore,
Now intermittent fasting is what we adore.

Copper lotas were left behind,
Now alkaline water is what we find.

Clay pots made way for steel and glass,
Now non-toxic cookware is back in class.

Cold baths were once a morning dread,
Now ice plunges refresh the head.

Yoga was just for monks in caves,
Now it's a global wellness wave.

Kadha was bitter, we made a face,
Now it's an immunity booster we all embrace.

Charcoal toothpaste, once a past trend,
Now activated charcoal is back again.

Joint families felt too tight,
Now co-living spaces feel just right.

Kirtans and bhajans, once dismissed,
Now sound healing tops the wellness list.

The things we ignored, the wisdom we strayed,
Are now the very things we wish had stayed.

What was "backward" is now "the trend,"
The wisdom of ages returns again.
Before we mock what elders say,
Remember - what's old may find its way.

Reflection: *What was once considered outdated is now a trend. Wisdom never truly disappears - it just gets rebranded.* **Are you valuing traditions only after the world reintroduces them to us?**

Come Home Before It's Too Late

They left with dreams packed in suitcases,
Hearts half empty, promises made -
"One day, I'll return."
One day became years, years became decades.

India became a story, a postcard,
A memory they never lived again.
They count in rupees, earn in dollars,
Still longing for simpler times.

Back home, they craved pasta and sushi,
Now, they spend fortunes for a taste of Indian spices.
Once they'd avoided the noise -
The drums, the neighbours, the chaos of family.

Now, in cold, quiet apartments,
They long for the uninvited guests,
The loud laughter, the voices that once annoyed them.
They set alarms for IST,

Watch cricket at dawn, hum anthem in a foreign land,
A single tear falling, surprising even them.

They search for India in street corners,
In temple bells ringing thousands of miles away.
But when they finally find time to return,
The door doesn't open like before.

The house is quieter.
Familiar voices don't call out their names.
And one chair at the dining table is forever empty.
Come home before it's too late.

My friend, take that flight, take that risk.
See your mother, hug your father, meet old friends.
Before time stamps your passport 'Too Late'
Instead of 'Arrived'.

A Note from the Author: *I have written this for friends and families who live abroad and often talk about coming back to India - someday. But that 'someday' keeps getting pushed further. They miss India, they miss home, yet life keeps them away. I hope this poem reminds them that doors don't stay open forever. If home is calling, don't wait too long to answer. Sometimes, later becomes never.*

A friend once shared a sobering truth—if you're in your 30s, visiting home once per year, you may only see your loved ones **around 30 more times**—maybe little more, maybe very less. When we count moments like this, the illusion of "plenty of time" fades quickly.

My friend, if there's someone waiting for you, don't wait too long to return.

The Chase that Never Ends

We are always chasing - success, validation, happiness. But does the race ever stop? This section explores the endless pursuit of "more" and asks whether we're running towards something meaningful or just running

Behind the Screens

How many hearts will be on my post,
When my story is shared the most?
They will comment, "Great job," with a smile,
But did they ever truly stay for a while?

On social feeds, we show only cheer,
Smiles and laughter, nothing unclear.
The dream vacation, the perfect day,
Edited, filtered, put on display.

We judge our lives by what we see,
Forgetting that online is not reality.
They share the joy, they hide the pain,
Yet we compare again and again.

Behind the screens, in silence deep,
Some hide their pain, some lose sleep.
What if they posted their worries and fear,
Would we still wish we had their year?

When the screens go dim, will the followers stay
Or will it be the ones who knew me every day?
So pause before you let yourself sink,
Not everything is real, so stop and think.

Reflection - *We seek likes, applause, and validation, forgetting that real joy isn't measured in numbers. True happiness comes from within.*
Are you living for approval or for ourselves? If applause fades tomorrow, will you still feel whole?

The Race That Never Ends

We chase the seats, the fame,
Fighting for what we think we claim.
A seat on the bus, a share in the fight,
A property, a promotion, all in sight.

But years will pass, and we'll look back,
Wondering if all we fought for was lack.
Why did we stress, why did we fight?
Was it worth it, this race we drove to survive?

Chasing tomorrow, we forget to live,
For the moments today that life can give.
So pause, take a breath, and ask yourself,
Is the race or fight worth the cost?

Because in the end, what really remains,
Is love, peace, and the joy that sustains.

Reflection - *We keep running - after money, promotions, and status. Sometimes, we even fight over property and* *possessions, believing they define us. But in the end, what do we really win? The real wealth is peace, not ownership.* **Are you chasing what matters, or just running in circles? Are you chasing life, or are you living it?**

Living Now

Life happens now. Yet, we are often too distracted to notice it. This section is a reminder to slow down, to be present, and to truly live before the moment slips away.

Captured, But Never Lived

We see something beautiful and bright,
But instead of living it, we grab the light.
Phones in hand, we click and snap,
Missing the moment, caught in the trap.

We store our photos, so many to see,
But how many times do we go back to them, truly?
We keep taking more, but they fade in time,
The real moment, left behind.

Yes, take one or two to capture the view,
But don't let the moment slip away from you.
We chase memories, click by click,
But in the end, life passes quick.

Why are we clicking, what's the real need?
To cherish a memory, or to feed the feed?
Are these moments for us to keep,
Or just for others, to scroll and peep?

So next time, put the phone down,
Don't keep staring at the screen all around.
For the memories that truly stay,
Are the ones we live fully, day by day.

Reflection - *We often try to save moments in our phones, but in doing so, we forget to live them. Life isn't meant to be stored; it's meant to be experienced.*
Are you capturing memories or missing them?

Happiness on Hold

We say, "I'll be happy when,
I get that job, or find my Zen."
"I'll smile more when I get that car,
Or when I travel, go so far."

But why wait for happiness to arrive?
It's something we can have, right here, alive.
It's in a hug, a smile, a peaceful night,
In little things that make life feel right.

So don't wait for some future day,
Choose happiness now, in your own way.
It's not far off, it's already near,
Waiting for you, right here.

Reflection - *We keep postponing happiness—when we get a job, when we travel, when we succeed. But happiness is only ever found in the now.* **What if joy was never meant to be a future event?**

The Noise We Fear

We wake up to sounds, loud and clear,
Rushing through the day, always in gear.
Phones, music, and the TV's light,
Always busy, day and night.

We scroll and tap, afraid to slow,
Silence feels empty, we never let go.
But have we ever stopped to hear,
The quiet voice that's always near?

A man once feared being alone,
So he filled his world with a noisy tone.
One day, the power went away,
No screens, no sounds, just peace to stay.

At first, he panicked, felt so small,
But then he noticed, he had it all.
The wind, the birds, his own heart beat,
A calm he'd missed, so pure, so sweet.

Silence is not empty, it's full of grace,
It holds the truth we need to face.
So take a break, and just be still,
We'll find the answers, if we will.

Reflection: *We fill our days with noise—music, messages, videos—so we don't have to sit in silence. But silence is not empty; it helps us hear our thoughts and understand ourselves better.*
When was the last time you sat quietly and listened to yourself? Are you listening to the world, or to yourself?

The Power of Now

Close this book, step outside,
Feel the air, watch the sky.
Life is waiting - don't let it pass by.

Reflection - *Every chase, every realisation, every reflection—brings us back to now. If these words made you pause, even for a moment, then perhaps that moment is where life truly happens. Not in the race, not in the past—only in this breath, this heartbeat, this now.*

Carry this Thought With You

Life is a constant **Race**, but in that rush, we often forget to pause. Every moment of stillness brings a **Reflection**, a chance to understand what truly matters. And through these moments, we reach a **Realisation** - that joy isn't in the chase, nor in what we leave behind, but in how we choose to live today

These words are not just mine; they belong to anyone who has ever questioned, reflected, or seen the truth hidden in everyday life. If even one poem made you stop and think, then this book has served its purpose. And if even one poem made you change something in your life, then its purpose has been fulfilled

The real race is with time, the true reflection is within, and the deepest realisation is to simply live.